The Pallikari of Nesmine Rifat

The Pallikari of Nesmine Rifat

David Solway

GOOSE LANE

Edited by Ross Leckie.
Cover design by Julie Scriver.
Book design by Julie Scriver and Lisa Rousseau.
Printed in Canada by AGMV Marquis.
10 9 8 7 6 5 4 3 2 1

Library and Archives Canada Cataloguing in Publication

Solway, David, 1941-
The pallikari of Nesmine Rifat / David Solway.

ISBN 0-86492-424-0

I. Title.

PS8537.O4P34 2005   C811'.54   C2004-907007-X

Published with the financial support of the Canada Council for the Arts, the Government of Canada through the Book Publishing Industry Development Program, and the New Brunswick Culture and Sports Secretariat.

Goose Lane Editions
469 King Street
Fredericton, New Brunswick
CANADA E3B 1E5
www.gooselane.com

for Eric Ormsby

Contents

11 Preface
12 Acknowledgements

Pallikari
17 Untitled
18 Sapphics on Fire
19 Refuge
20 Threnody
21 Queries
22 The Lie, the Truth
23 Fear
24 Godmother
25 Letter to the Wife
26 Dictynna
27 The Gloss
28 We Always Drank Greek Brandy
29 Colloquy of Equals
30 The Secret History
31 A Reply
32 Denial
33 My Love
34 Love
35 The Thirteenth Fairy
36 A Matter of Taste
37 A Letter of Self-Justification
38 The Black Book
39 Blue Mountain.com
40 Ancient Guzelyurt
41 A French Lesson
42 Mnasidika
43 A Question

44 Sequel

45 Curious

46 Unentitled

47 Works and Days

48 The Brand

49 Pantoum

50 Prime Minister of Cyprus

51 Temenos

52 The Apple

53 The Teacher

54 Alcaics

55 Correspondence

56 A Ghazal for Two Houses

57 A Warning

58 Where the Bed Is

59 A Letter Imagined

60 The Way Ahead

62 A Difference

63 Karaghiozis

64 A Letter Anticipated

65 From the "Garland of Sulpicia"

66 Wind

67 Postscript

71 Afterword

73 Notes

76 Glossary of Greek and Turkish terms

ت

Preface

Nesmine Rifat was born in Istanbul in 1965 and currently lives in Guzelyurt, a village in Turkish Cyprus. Her last book of poems, *Resistances*, appeared in 1987, followed by two prose chapbooks dealing with political themes, *The Imprisoned Muse* in 1993 and *Manacles and Fetters* in 1998. She dedicated *Pallikari* to the fisherman-poet Andreas Karavis, a native of Crete: "for Andreas, whose existence remains a mystery." This accounts for her occasional use of Greek terms.

Acknowledgements

I wish to thank Nesmine Rifat for providing me with the occasional exegesis and prose crib and for tolerating my at times indiscreet questions. I am also grateful to Yunus Emre for his timely help with the more intractable elements of the Turkish original.

Several of these poems appeared in the Turkey Issue of *Descant* in the summer of 2003.

Pallikari

Nesmine Rifat

Yurdunu sevmeliymis insan
Oyle diyor hep babam
Benim yurdum
Ikiye bolunmus ortasindan
Hangi yansini
Sevmeli insan

(My father says
Love your homeland
My homeland
Is divided into two
Which part should I love?)
— Nese Yasin

butun isin gucun yasamak olacak

(living must be your whole occupation)
— Nazim Hikmet

Untitled

Ah my love, my lost one, my Andreas, my *pallikari*,
my hero who refuses laurels,
my fisher of fish and of women
whose nets sing lyrical with prey,
my pirate of letters and lockets,
my warrior whose weapons are implements of persuasion,
my poet whose words are tempered in coals
and hardened in water,
whose sweet petitions lodge in the heart
and cannot be removed,
my shedder of titles and pretensions for this is love,
my bearded elder in a young man's form,
my lion of stone reposing on the lintel,
my hermit in whose cave a seafarer shelters,
my Captain of Caiques who welcomes the storm,
my dancer of *rebetika* and lord of the handkerchief,
my leaper whose feet can pilfer the silk from a woman's hair,
my defier of the gods with the grin of an urchin,
ah my love, my Andreas, my pirate, my *pallikari*,
my friend, my enemy,
my visitor in Cyprus who crossed the line,
heal the rift between our peoples in my body
that opens in the night like a flower of darkness
and awaits the invasion of love.

Envy and vehemence inflame my spirit,
Longing and deprivation burn my body,
And I am reduced to embers in the grate,
    Thin smoke in the flue.

Remembering the fires of consummation
That annealed both body and spirit like glass
And healed the crack in the substance of desire,
    I am still aghast.

I will burn the books where your name is inscribed.
I will throw these photographs into the flames.
And I linger at the hearth empty and cold,
    A guest like Sappho.

Refuge

When one finds oneself communing with one's shadow,
when the house one lives in has become a museum
and its occupant a disconsolate curator
attending to the usual exhibits,
when the sunset has been drained of colour,
when the river's impetuous rush is now a languid current
meandering nowhere in particular,
when the birds discover they have misplaced their song sheets
and lapse into bewildered silence,
when lurid sentiment pours in
to drown the spirit and ruin the furniture,
when the body begs to be violated and yet bars its doors securely,
when one posts letters without stamps or addresses
and every barbed indictment goes unanswered
or cannot find its target,
the only refuge to be had are little rooms
lit by candles stored for when the power fails
one visits late at night in solitude.

You once likened my nipples
to little pink soldiers standing at attention;
another time to tiny minarets
and also slender finials
glittering on their sunlit domes;
then they were half-olives
studded in their loaves;
again, burnt almonds glazed with sugar;
now, flushed with kisses,
petite odalisques voluptuous on their bolsters.
You could never get over my nipples,
these pale and embittered widows
you once sucked the colour into,
one mourning the poet,
the other the lover.
I stroke them tenderly with my fingertips
which have been dipped in brandy
and cured in the smoke of cigarettes
to arouse the memory of your lips
and comfort them in their bereavement.

What did you fall in love with when you met her?
Was it her name,
the perfect palindrome that brought you dutifully back
to the port you had put out from,
my poet charmed by the alphabet?
Was she prettier than me,
more loving, more complaisant, more devoted?
Did her love cries sing in your ears
more melodious than mine
or the tip of her tongue alliterate more tenderly
your uvulars and labials?
Were her nectars sweeter than the elixirs of my body?
Did she prepare a better *djoumboushi* for your table
than the lavish trestles I set out for you?
And were her eggs richer in the yolk than mine?
Tell me, O my fickle one, betrayer of the word
you swore you would be faithful to,
was it power or helplessness that seduced you,
my *pallikari* in everything but deed?

It has been said that a woman
is born of the rib of a man;
that she has been shaped by his will
from the common clay of need
to be his receptacle, his utensil;
that she is the servant in the garden,
the attendant who squats by the tripod
to cook or to prophesy,
handmaid to his imperial whim,
secretary to his pentecostal ravings,
his sacrifice at Aulis.
For my sisters I refute this libel.
But for myself I acknowledge an admonishing truth
and live in the epic he has written
of journeys and conquests and returns,
the mistress strolling on the parapet
and the wife unweaving her nights by the fire.

Do you remember how once you stood above me
like a straddling colossus or a god
as I lay beneath you in the half-filled tub,
and how you let your golden rain
play along my collar-bone
and sleek its passage down between my breasts
to splash upon my belly's taut terrain
and rill within the clefts and gullies
of my most secret places?
That was one of the many ways
in which you claimed me.
Now I am yours beyond deliverance or revolt
and yours beyond
whatever may be left of my poor dignity,
always dreading what is yet to come,
like Danae giving birth to oracles.

Godmother

I plead with you, my love,
let me be godmother to the young *pallikari*,
let me fasten this tiny golden cross about his neck,
let me anoint his head with tears.
My womb is empty of lineage,
my breasts without milk
though my flesh is pliant and scented with musk
and my thighs like a cradle
impatient for happiness.

If only to be close to him again,
  the *pallikari* you have taken from me,
I, who have never touched a woman, would
  welcome you to my bed.

I would kiss the mouth that he has kissed,
  suckle at the breasts of my rival,
caress her belly and flanks with delight
  and enter the secrets she has shared.

I would braid her tresses with little coloured beads,
  sprinkle her linens with perfumes.
I would rub her flesh with oils from the bath
  and entwine my limbs with hers.

If only to be close to him again,
  the *pallikari* you have stolen from me,
I would kneel at your feet in gratitude
  and drink his brimmings from your cup.

Dictynna

Poor Britomartis
who, escaping from King Minos,
leaped over a cliff into the sea
and was caught in a fisherman's net.
For that reason she is also called Dictynna,
from *dictyon* for "net"
as you well know,
you who are both king and fisherman,
Minos and Andreas, hook and net,
while I remain a captive
by any name.

It has its own divinity, a tense,
quick and tender roughness at the tip,
the subtle nib of an intelligence
beyond the commonplace. I watch it dip,
poke, quiver, scribbling its glossary
on chosen parchment with the flourish
of instinctual calligraphy
and medieval diligence. Though flesh,
no monk's or scholar's pen has ever worked
so earnestly at an illustration,
a rosy rubric or an abstruse text
or exegesis of the three-in-one
as his most sweet and angel-feathered quill;
no holy implement articulate
with truer dedication, higher will,
the triple pleasures of the reprobate.

We always drank Greek brandy — coarse, no-star Metaxa was his favourite; as a concession to me, he jettisoned his Karelia and smoked pungent Turkish ovals. We were tolerant of one another's redeeming vices. As for virtues, he had none, but rather qualities and passions. As for virtues, he could never forgive me mine. And he would always grow a little irritated when I quoted him my favourite stanza from Yunus Emre:

> *Knowledge is to understand,*
> *To understand who you are.*
> *If you know not who you are*
> *What's the use of learning?*

I know who I am. And I know, too, who he is. I have learned him to the letter and the fraction. I send him this slight but heartfelt bit of doggerel to signal my belated wisdom with pretend insouciance.

> *And you were on your way, way before I knew it.*
> *Although the privateer and minstrel rarely tarries,*
> *it was nothing I was able to intuit.*
> *Now I know. Such is the way of* pallikaris.

Colloquy of Equals

Perhaps I have been too outspoken, love.
A woman must prevent her tongue, we're told,
or speak with modesty and grace,
or hover like a toy kolibri at her master's lips,
sipping at his wisdom,
or nibble the berries of his words
like a timorous bird that flutters in the hedge.
But this was never my way.
I speak to you direct and plain,
am lewd and candid, genital and salt,
neither hiding my desire nor pretending moderation.
I am your equal in all our colloquies of body and of speech
and when I have deferred to your imperium
it was by choice and not by nature or by rule.
But now that I have lost you, I fear
perhaps I have outspoken my own good.
And yet I am your equal, love,
a *pallikari* in a woman's mind,
and no frail creature buffeted by the wind.

I am rich with secrets, with copious
intensities of hidden things, with joys
remembered and suppressed, and the stunned poise
of someone who has read Procopius

to disengage, from deep within, the facts.
All blood is tainted and all flesh corrupt,
the viands mingled where an empress supped
with strange, exotic aphrodisiacs.

I am your cast off queen, your minion,
the secret deep within your nuptials
who shall emerge one day to roam your halls.
I shall betray you like Justinian.

A Reply

That night upon the deck of your caique
you called me your Turkish Delight,
sampling my *loukoumia* with your tongue
or tippling at my breasts,
and let me taste the honey from your jar,
so thick and sweet it had to be from Crete.
And then at last you entered me
as if I were the garden
you said you'd once been banished from,
the Gnostic serpent coupling with its dream.
And then you danced among the wicker tappit hens
while I clapped time and drew you with my gaze.

I feel the skin of memory pull and tauten
and fit itself precisely to my days —
the skin you shed to make yourself anew,
to slip and glisten in a stranger's grove
and vanish in the gleaming dark of love.

But I remember what you have forgotten.

Denial

What comes from denial?
The understanding of fate?
The valedictory smile?
The chance to sublimate?

Granted it is no sublime
regard, but raw desire
at the unsuitable time —
why extinguish the fire

that nibbles at the gut?
And is it any less
for kindling at the root
and not at kindredness?

I call down curses on your grizzled pate —
may you rot at the bottom of the sea —
as I, who could have been your daughter, wait
to be the wife you would not make of me.

May the storm crush you in the narrow strait
where the clashing rocks seize their prey and grind.
May the fish nibble at your bones like bait
and feast upon the eyes that made me blind.

You, who could have been my father, instead
the subtle tempter grey as I was green,
may Charon take you who conducts the dead.
(I write this out of love for you.) Nesmine.

He holds the dying creature in his shirt
and a tense unreality afflicts
the one bewildered sense of what is right
or wrong or just appropriate, and sticks
in the air like a smell. Supper is late
this evening. The abandoned kitten licks
uselessly at the dropper as we wait
there, knowing it must be killed. The clock leaks
time like milk but does not nourish it. It's
not the dying cat I mean, but something
else that summons us to act when little fits
the ancient protocols to which we cling
or clears indebtedness. To call it quits,
we must kill from love, or it is nothing.

Let the next one be a girl.
May she come with freckles
to remind you daily of my face
and may her hair crimp up with curls.
You will not be let off easily.
Let her ruffle your Hellenic sensibility.
May you struggle to provide the dowry
and focus your attention on purity and trouble,
frisk her suitors for their intentions.
May your wife form reactionary alliances
to remind you of the other side.
And when dawn relinquishes to dusk
may your daughter vex you with a Turkish *pallikari*
who seduces her with verses,
then abandons her to alien consummations.
For there is such a thing as justice in this world
that bides upon the generations
and is only a matter of time.

You say I never loved you
but only loved the nights that you could fill
with melodies and recitations
and certain indiscreet devotions,
O my prodigy of labial explorations
who could articulate a little gland with dithyrambs
and probe the inlets of my reticence.
Ah yes, my love, you knew exactly how
to bring a woman's body to the pitch
of lamentation for having to reenter dailiness.
And yet the words that tumbled from your lips
I never sundered from their candied ministrations
nor severed from the intellect I loved
that sweetly metred out its couplets
knowing all too well the world's bitterness.
To say I never loved you
betrays your own intemperate compulsions,
you who were addicted to my taste
as remedy for all you found acerbic.
I say you never loved me
but only loved what pleased your appetite,
the chocolate of proscribed communions,
the minim cake of honey-macaroon,
the tang of orange water,
the cinnamon that tingled on your tongue.

What choice have you given me, my heartless larcenist?
For when you left you took away with you
the lovers who might have solaced me,
have made my nights bearable,
laved me with ambergris and civet,
brought flasks of sweet nepenthe to my mouth.
You have emptied the world of assuagements,
deprived me of the desire for another,
of the power to imagine another as you,
to imagine you as another,
to let the night draw a curtain over recognition.
Because I slept beside you once,
now I sleep with eyes wide open.
And so I beg you to be compassionate,
to permit me to be touched
by the only creature in this world
with whom I can still be intimate.

"I wish to be another, therefore I am,"
said Orhan Pamuk, who is himself
encrypted in his *Black Book*
as I am written in the very shadow
of your pen. Is
this not a sign of occult complicities?
These are my insignia:
the scent of my skin released like a rubbed herb
by your curious fingers,
the cries you swore were graven in your soul,
the bright intelligence you said was mine.
Now I wish to be another
to be no other than the one I am,
the missing wife who sings a smile to your lips,
and not the one whom you have written
off, the dream whose meaning
has escaped you, cloaked in your black books
like a secret name you utter without knowing it.

Fairooz. Ahmed. Sherafa. Aladdin. Mirick.
These are the names that cluster in the Trojan Horse
someone left parked at my gate,
each descending from its belly
armed with a greeting card from Blue Mountain,
a host of mercantile corsairs,
every one infected by a virus —
the Backdoor virus, as it happens —
and every inch of my electric acres
serving as a peneplain
for this vast Blue Mountain Range that ridged up overnight
hard as marble and dolomite
and studded with crusader castles
to plug the gaps and passes
(much like the Kyrenia Range but minus transverse faults).
Now you need no longer block my messages,
my troubling greeting cards
cannot scale these peaks and lowering crags.
I must content myself with the loving depredations
of my swarm of precipice providers,
Fairooz and Ahmed, Sherafa, Aladdin and Mirick,
here in the foothills of the Blue Mountains
which have obliterated all my old horizons.

Unlike the city of Si-il-lu
larger and more splendid than me
I rose against a foreign master
and was brutally suppressed.
Some time later
my harbour silted up,
my olives felled that yielded jars of sweetest oil
and my copper mines shut down.
Soon I was destroyed by Arab raids.

In my tumbledown Acropolis
silver and gold bracelets were unearthed,
a clay figurine blackened by fire,
a frieze representing the war of the Amazons
and coins bearing stamps of Marion, Paphos and Lapithos.

Once there was a settlement here,
nothing like Si-il-lu, yet
for all it humbleness pleasing and industrious:
a deep, protected harbour, fertile soil
and underground cisterns cut into the rock.
Not for nothing was I named *Morphou*,
"the beautiful place."
Now I am known as *Toumba Tou Skouru*,
that is, "Mound of Darkness."
You will find my remnants
in the Archeological and Natural Science Museum
in modern Guzelyurt,
my pottery yours to inspect from a distance,
the White Slip ware and the Base Ring ware, both.

Now we've got English out of the way
(you were never much good at it)
and Turkish has always defeated you,
let me kiss your oils, love,
coop my chevalier in a militant embrace,
decorate you with epaulettes of maiden blush
as I march down the field of glory
toward your tricolor of red and white and tan,
nuzzle my nez nicely in your beaupers,
French you fine in my travelling argot,
offer you parole to roam in my devotions
and give you the gift of tongues,
especially the tongue of triumph and seduction,
to diversify your monoglot demotic.

There will be no more men
to knead my supple flesh, to claim my sweet attentions,
my lingering looks and probing fingers.
And since I am no longer adequate to myself,
I will sing the song of Bilitis now
and find my lovely Mnasidika
whose braids I will plait with flowers
as I would have done your wedded lady's once,
dimple scent of lemon and pomegranate
on her delicate lobes
and in the dewy under-crease
there where the pendant bosom meets the rib,
I will sense her knees rise up behind me
to enclose me in the fragrance of her garden
and let me season my delight
in the spiciness of her little bush,
I will turn her about on my bed
and bend and kiss the tiny dell
in the comely small of her back,
O my tongue will speak her every mystery.
For I will banish you entirely with intimacies
you cannot imagine or approve,
I will send you packing with curious estrangements,
I will break your composure with depravities,
you who have driven me to delirium
and into the arms of my lovely Mnasidika.

A Question

I see myself now snakelike
starting at the upraised ankle,
sliding up the inside of her thighs
as she spreads her legs in anticipation,
her petals all aflutter.
I will millimetre my kisses toward her little flowerpot
(even stop for a moment
to whisper in her ear my intentions),
then trace each petal with the tip of my tongue
and sip the moistness that has formed there,
let it lickle in along the length of me.
You will in the meantime note
how my breasts hang laden
from their lissome bough
like rounded nippled apples for you to nibble at
and even bite
if the urge to sweetness overtakes you.
But should you fail to be tempted
then I will move sly and sinuous
to where I imagine you lying by our side
and entice you irresistibly
to gather from my mouth what I have eaten.
Would this break you, then, you so aloof,
so newly cold to our loveship,
so banished in your solemn rectitude?

Sequel

Her name was not Mnasidika but Guneli.
She looked so much like me
she might have been my very twin.
I met her in the marketplace,
gradually we became friends,
then companions sharing a kindred history,
soon we were confidantes, eventually more than this.
And so I sampled from her provender
what you had amply savoured of my own,
the loaves and melons of a woman's flesh,
the tentativeness of a woman's mouth,
the caverns of forgetfulness
where for a sheltered night or two
I was no longer discontented.
But ah! when the blue-embroidered yellow robe
Guneli let fall as I approached her once
revealed my image in a living glass,
I was no longer who I was but *you*
advancing on your willing prey,
the man who pillaged me of every good,
plundered my orchard, stripped me clean,
and left me nothing but the two of us again.

ت

Curious

You are curious, then,
my prurient one, my palatal adventurer!
Hers was a flowery taste.
It reminded me of rosewater
or of the honey that fills the flowers of the field thistle
and of how as children we sucked the honey
out of each tiny narrow oval-shaped purple petal.
And I remember how her lips swelled,
pouted and glistened, grew thick and heavy,
when I chased the honey to its innermost chamber.
You will have known this too, my departed lover,
but never, never as I have.

What makes you think that you are now entitled
to all that you denied your former love?
Is opulence and joy to be your lot,
a plump caique laden with the catch
you merely cast your nets to haul back in?
A vineyard sprouting rich with sun-flushed grapes
you crushed with dancing feet to fill your vats?
And in your bed the lithe and yielding flesh
that heaps up blessings offered without sweat
except what fills the pores with oil or sap
or honeys forth its sweetness at your touch?
What makes you think you need not sow nor reap
but granaries will burst at your behest?
That every word will summon home a world?
What makes you think that you are now entitled
by right of deprivation to my crops?
My love, my love, my love, forgive my love,
I grant you freely all that you have taken,
I give my love although my fields are bare.

Works and Days

I suppose I never knew you well
or well enough to know that what you craved
was more than I was able to confer:
the staple long hexameters of daily life
that you could raise your epithets upon.
You came to me for lyric merriments,
for sweet digressions in the Lydian mode,
for swift, acerbic epigrams,
for tight quatrains and nimble, headlong recitations.
You did not come to me for pastoral or chronicle.
Victim of the strophe and the line,
how could I have known
your deep suspicion of the shorter poem
or of the poet's fugitive performance,
purveyor of ephemeral felicities?
It was another rhythm that you sought
beyond the metric built into my bones
to lay the groundwork for your solitary figurations,
the ode and epic of your works and days.

I marvel now how memory is stored
in all the body's skins and envelopes,
the tongue that holds another's speech intact,
the throat that shelters a profound declension,
the breast a palimpsest of many tendernesses,
the belly like a strip of parchment for notations,
the navel a hollow where messages are kept,
and the vellum of love's confluence that records
the intimate confessions of the soul.
But most I marvel
how the body bears no prejudice,
holds no surface or declivity apart,
and how it offers up its many selves
to be imprinted by another,
remembering even in its darkest, vaulted privacy
the keenest of all violations,
the delve and thrust of intimate possessing,
the brand of love that marked me as your own.

Pantoum

So many ways of being elegant,
feigning nonchalance, dissipating gloom —
a poem arrayed in scraps, as if unmeant,
or stylishly archaic: the pantoum.

I loved you then in all my early bloom
while you, my teacher, scorched me with your fire,
and all my little instruments made room
to domicile the kindlings of your lyre.

That was then. Now the flame is on the pyre,
the spark of Spring has flickered into Fall,
grown sparse as your beloved Shakespeare's choir,
Sonnet 73, if you recall.

Well, I am older, like those once-loved dolls,
ragged and weathered, cruelly set adrift
to crowd the attic of memorials.
But I have learned the lessons of your gift.

Forgive your clever pupil — don't be miffed —
if now she speaks of love and love's intent
to make the doubtful teacher's eyebrow lift.
Accept her chic antique. And be content.

ﺖ

Andreas, you have my vote
for Prime Minister of Cyprus
to replace the aged reptile
who currently presides.

You would not bring order,
the economy would collapse,
the girls reinforce their crinolines,
the workers take to the street.

And yet you have my vote
for Prime Minister of Cyprus
for you would bind our peoples in
one great union of resentment:

at your runic convolutions,
your indifference to the common weal,
and your mocking of the office
of Prime Minister of Cyprus.

Tell me love, how is it
that shyness and timidity can be put to flight
so easily, with such effortless dispatch,
that I who blushed at an overheard remark
or at a stranger's unanticipated glance
could hear myself cry out unlearned profanities,
be rude and ribald, perform the tenderest atrocities,
that I who quailed once
before the terrifying splendour of encounters
and turned away to guard my frailty
could suddenly put to rout all seemliness,
become epitome of concubines
allowing you to plumb my cyprinid vicinities,
become the living incarnation of the Empress Theodora
hungry for incursions,
eager to betray propriety,
assassin of every rectitude,
surrendering all my territories to your marauding usurpations
from the *temenos* of my spirit
down to my subclitoral demesnes?

The Apple

Can you find it in you now that time
demands I put hostilities to rest
and call a truce between our warring bloods
to pardon me the mischief I have done,
I who have reversed the myth
and offered you the Apple of Contention
to spread confusion in your crennellated tower
and flood your mouth with dreams of succulence?
And yet I know that this can never be
and that, if I am to be true to love,
I cannot beg this last indemnity.
I know that time's the wound that never heals,
that opens always in the pitched, embattled Now,
and that apples never cease to redden on the bough.

You taught that love
brought all the senses into play.
You commanded "Spread!"
and I opened myself wholly to your relishing.
Nor do I exaggerate when I say
that my idea of the infinite
came from the measure of the joy
you brought into the littleness of my life
in every radiant sense:
the ardour of the soul hugging its own flesh
and the swelling of a small parochial world
into something hued and lit and manifold.

Now as I watch you
stiffen into one dimension
I have come to understand
you are a destiny grown rigid.
You are a stretch of perished time.
And as you recede, O my mentor,
into the consummated dark
you have become the measure of my deprivation,
the measure of my craft.
You have brought me back into the world.
You have taught me limits.

Alcaics

You would prefer *this* form no doubt, being Greek
to the very door, the table and the bed,
    your hair still black and your sinews firm
    though verdigris and slack are starting now,

you'll note, to work their foreign sorcery in
for all the contrary magic you've invoked.
    The truss of tight-cinched words will falter —
    and this despite your arsenic hauteurs.

Thus forms dissolve within their incarnations
and strong alcaics diminish in the flesh.
    Yet in such archaic, male modes you
    strut, you who can admit and bear no doubt.

Correspondence

I do not like these days when I awaken
without a dream from you,
when I arise in an unfamiliar room
doubled over with the cramp of your absence
(which you would welcome since it gives you an advantage),
mornings when the poste restante is empty
and I rummage for a scrap of minor history,
a letter, a note, a cryptic address for a ghostly assignation,
a small memento of the night —
it seems that this is what I have been given
not more of.
I awaken in this town which has been violently
chopped in half and pockmarked
with the scars of a previous combat,
barbed wire strung along the green line.
It is terribly hot here.
Though something in us no longer corresponds,
please tell me where to send the postcards from Lefkosa.

The nest I made for you is emptiness.
Just look about. There's little left to bless

except for a derelict shell become
unlivable. And by this barren place

the black river you sailed away upon
flows sluggish from the quartered darkness

whose last inhabitant composes this,
the sullen line, the word's fragmented trace.

Such is the landscape you prepared for me,
the scene of desolation, and the house

beside the river that you loved — the house
that's now abandoned to the wilderness.

My name's upon the house where I now dwell,
the NESt not MINE, the RIver FAThomless.

A Warning

You have been forewarned:
do not take me lightly.
Come one more time into my bed
and I will make a meal of you.
I will unravel the seam of your pouch
and have you with my morning coffee,
unstitch the cicatrix upon your abdomen
and fry you up as an exotic specialty.
My mouth waters in anticipation.
Make no mistake about this.
I will leech you of your last sustaining essence,
drain you of your vital distillations
and leave you elderly and parched
as if upon a slab.
Do not forget my passion for the visceral.
Do not deprecate my hunger.
Do not underestimate my bite.

I used to get there
just by gazing into your eyes.
I would arrive at my destination
merely in reverie or anticipation,
imagining you entering the room.
And to know that I had pleased you
was all the sustenance I needed.

Now I am taking myself back.
I will travel elsewhere
or if it comes to that
arrive at the same destination
by other means.
I will nourish myself on ginger instead of honey.

Why should this not be possible?
So much of it is in the mind
and after all
that is where the bed is.

"Do not mistake me for a latter-day Othello.
As much as you may play the innocent Desdemona
dismantled by conspiracies
you yourself have sown
to pique my interest
and prick my armour of assumed indifference,
I will not respond with pillows
or take your breath away with jealousy.
That handkerchief which I so loved and gave thee
as you remember from my dancing days
you may bestow on any chosen paramour.
And though I still recall
with undiminished want
your every subtle detail of dialogue and demeanour
I will not tread again
the soft proscenium of your intricate temptations,
neither for love nor vengeance,
as much as I may play the striding lord."

ت

TEMPLE OF PIGATHES THIS WAY
In the western courtyard there is
a square altar which resembles
a small stepped pyramid with a truncated top.
shouldn't read while driving
one lonely planet beside another
YUKARI CAMI (LEVKA)
OPEN TO VISITORS
a green blur melds with ochre
and a wash of burnt umber
staining the glass
my shield against a moving world
remember this
ST. MAMAS MONASTERY
the patron saint of tax evaders
my kind of saint
saving the lamb he rode the lion into the capital
and was absolved of debt
During the Middle Ages
cluster of limes
inadvertent eye rhymes
no a carillon of limes shedding music in the bright air
a building in the Gothic style was added
cypress oak pine eucalyptus
to the original structure.
was there ever an original structure
this is always how it is
no pure architecture orders our lives
we are a chaos of competing styles
assembled ruins afterthoughts
the world streaming by

In the eighteenth century a dome was erected.
like the sweating stones of Byzantine chapels
the sarcophagus oozes balm
against diseases of the soul
and also calms a turbulent sea
remember this too
KARAVAS 25 KILOMETRES.
can one letter make a difference
look elsewhere
look
red and white stars of the cistus
is there anything lovelier
than juniper and pistachio in flower
yes cyclamen and narcissus and the blood of poppies
PIRI OSMAN PASHA MOSQUE
the wooden iconostasis was painted blue and gold
the lower part carved of marble
burgeoning with figs grapes and acorns
FAMAGUSTA →
VISIT THE CASTLE OF OTHELLO
thou teachest me Minion your dear lies dead
but who is the victim
no escaping
CAPE APOSTOLOS ANDREAS
This rugged spit of land
commands the eastern Mediterranean
and is a natural fortification.
Entire navies have come to grief here.
forget this
forget this

ت

A Difference

There was a difference there,
too much space around my tongue
to make me feel at home
or that I was in some way part of him.

It did not look like it was bursting
to breach my channels
but rather like a proud and happy wavelet
or curved like a fibrous daffodil.

On the palate it was olive oil,
thin and slightly off,
lacking the jammy thickness
you once would coat me with.

Later, when it came his turn
to practise these devotions,
I did not feel his teeth as I did yours,
as I still do.

And I did not feel beautiful
with my smudged mascara
that never hid my freckles,
as once I did with you.

Karaghiozis

What gnaws at me, what saves me
friends and enemies, I could raise them
nicely, on my dreadful shoulders.
"Like Karaghiozis," Dionysis Savvopoulos

None of this has happened as it should.
For I am captive still
in a theatre of gestures,
a puppet show of dreams and shadows.
I flicker like a wraith in a hall of theorems,
an underworld of dissevered shades.
My eyes darken in your absence,
my knees part in reminiscence,
my veiled ducts moisten in my thoughts of you
with tears of longing,
my hands form empty cups
for the weight of your slung delectables,
my fingertips ache with a lost impress.
Now I consummate my love in cold displacements,
always a little ridiculous,
like a projection on the screen
of your favourite *Karaghiozis*.

"Not to be undone, I too remember
how you cupped me like a brandy glass,
lit my manhood like a tall candle,
how your fingers worked like knives and forks,
how your shapely legs
clamped and pinioned me in place,
and how you turned me in your mouth
like an expert taster
and rendered judgment only with your appetite.
My dear Nesmine
I have learned at your slender feet
how the predator may be transformed
into the prey,
the devourer into the object of another's feasting,
the body opened to sustain
the fantasy of weakness,
the Lion of St. Mark rent by the lamb
or dominated by the meekest saint.
Forgive me, princess, if I have forfeited
the pleasures of your table and your bed
but I have done so only
not to be undone."

Ah Cerinthus, let me save you from those twisted nets that beset the
hunter,
the thorns and brambles that have pierced you, entangled you as if
in chains,
let your lost Sulpicia keep you safe from the teeth that rend your
unsuspecting flesh
and from the subtler snares of sweet regard that tear you from the
world.
Do not let my body waste away or shed its colour and its strength,
my hair grow lank and grey from tribulation,
and I will hold my tears for some dark day when you are hard to
please,
I who offer for your sake unending supplications
though you may utter blasphemies from Hell or practise cruelties of
silence.
I pray that when you think of me your pulses rouse.
Know this: without me there is no loving.
Observe the law the goddess sets
for I, Sulpicia, am her most dedicated votary.
And should some hussy now usurp my place
may she be clawed to shreds and bloody tatters by maddened
ravening beasts
while you, unworthy as you are, escape unharmed.
Since it is your pleasure, I will let you hunt without reproach,
Cerinthus,
protected by my charms and invocations, my rites and vigils,
but only if you promise to return to your long-suffering one,
teach her what you have learned on the slopes and in the coverts,
renew your pleasures in her all-forgiving arms.

Wind

What can resist the wind?
The trees are in deep prayer.
Snowflakes, like schools of tiny fish,
switch direction every few moments
as if evading predators.
It's the wind,
the wind, that compels
either to supplication or to flight.
Who can repel the wind?

No doubt I have exhausted you
with my incessant clamourings and perpetual voracities,
my *Anaphora Ston Andrea*,
these longings of the groin and mind,
my calling out to you as if you were a draegerman
to come and find me in the sinuous dark I live in,
to hear my voice crying in the rubble of my days
and pull me from the ruin about my head;
wearied you with threats and imprecations
and the curse of my continued presence;
haunted you with phantoms of the bed
where long ago you frisked and plunged
like a dolphin in the rumpled seafoam,
revelling in a cold ancestral innocence,
the tart impersonality of desire.
No doubt I have oppressed you with endearments
and punished you with tributes,
troubled your vocation with anceps and Adonics,
heaped you over with honey and invective,
walked through every silence like an open door,
treated each refusal as an invitation,
afflicted you with changes of internal weather,
one day avenging crone, the next submissive maid.
Professing faith, unfaithful by deflection,
connoisseuse of amorous desecrations,
proud to claim Olympian descent,
no doubt I have become too much for you
(perhaps I always was)
and more than you can handle with your customary flair,
like that other Cyprian

who skimmed the painted coasts of my familiar lair,
hair writhing in a fatal wind,
succubus to dismay your dreams and suck you dry.
I sense, my love, I sense it now no less than you.
And if I only could
I too would turn a deaf ear to my tedious entreaties,
break the lure of carnal immolations,
and standing on my shell, aristocratic and perverse,
kick the scallop from beneath my feet
and live with you away from me at last.

ﺕ

Afterword

I owe my acquaintance with Nesmine Rifat to a number of enigmatic allusions in the work of Andreas Karavis, whose *Saracen Island* I translated from the Greek in the years 1998 to 2000, and to the good offices of my friend, the poet and Islamic scholar Eric Ormsby, who met my new correspondent at a literary conference in Istanbul. (See my *An Andreas Karavis Companion*, pp. 48-49.) My only knowledge of her actual practice at the time was a translation of an obscure Karavis poem entitled "Faith" (*Pístis* in Greek, *Inanç* in Turkish) from her 1987 *Resistances*, sent to me first by Ormsby and later by Karavis critic and biographer Constantine Makris in the original Greek when I was working on *Saracen Island*. (See Makris *The Wild Emerald: The Poetry of Andreas Karavis*.) To be sure, "Pístis" was a rather modest effort, but what surprised me was that I found Rifat's version of the piece superior to the original both in its directness of address and in its metaphorical allusiveness. These are, it is true, qualities that Rifat's poetic voice and timbre share with that of her paramour, but there is also a strong and intimately personal inflection which one looks for in vain in Karavis and that renders her poetry not only more accessible on the whole but also, if one can put it this way, somehow more *lovable*. She perhaps lacks the thematic amplitude we find in Karavis, but for many readers this ellipsis of overall effect is recompensed by the intimacy of her appeal. In any case, my curiosity was piqued by these events, but Karavis preserved an invincible reticence when I queried him about his connection to Rifat. No doubt his recent marriage to Anna Zoumi had something to do with his reserve.

I first wrote to Rifat in a bid to discover what I could about her mysterious relationship with the Greek poet, but in the course of our exchange I began to learn more about her own poetry. I soon formed the notion of collaborating with her on a translation of her

ت

work or at least those portions of her material which she considered relatively translatable in the hands of a novice like myself. This was how I came into the possession of her as yet unpublished divan, *Pallikari*, which served the double purpose of filling in many of the of the gaps in my knowledge of the relationship between Karavis and Rifat and of exposing me to the fresh and candid quality of her own creative urge, which, at least in my estimation, rivals that of her former mentor and lover.

Pallikari furnishes an ongoing record of the author's changing reactions and emotions in the wake of a failed love affair, giving the impression of a work in progress or a fluid documentary whose conclusion cannot be foreseen at its inception. This is what Rifat in a letter to me called "process poetry": a sort of transcript keeping pace with events as they unfold. In its later stages often ontradicting its earlier assertions, it represents a poetic project that annot be planned or conceived in advance of its execution. There is a sense, then, in which the divan can never reach "closure" but can only be cut off at some arbitrary point. The "Postscript" may eventually serve as a new salutation.

And indeed this is what seems to be happening, as Rifat has now embarked on a continuation of her "project," drafting a series of poems written from the point of view of a male poet, in this case Karavis himself, who insists on practising a kind of poetic impenitence and recounting the story of abandonment from his own perspective. Two examples, "A Letter Imagined" and "A Letter Anticipated," appear in this collection, but with so little evidence at my disposal I am obviously in no position to comment on the viability of this latest enterprise. It certainly represents one way of extending the divan, but all this reposes problematically in the future.

ﺕ

"Untitled": line 11 is a direct citation from an Andreas Karavis poem, "On Karpathos." The handkerchief (line 16) links the lead dancer to the other members of the popular circle dance or kalamatiano.

"Queries": this poem was clearly inspired by an Andreas Karavis prose poem, "Falling in Love (for Anna)," which appeared in the literary journal *Elladas* (Athens, Spring 2002).

"Fear": according to Greek myth, Danae was imprisoned by her father, King Acrisius of Argos, to circumvent an oracle which warned him that his daughter's son would cause his death. She was visited by Zeus in the form of a golden shower and duly impregnated.

"Godmother": The godparent is a venerable institution in Greece, where it is taken far more seriously than in the West. Rifat's request would be considered as bordering on sacrilege.

"Dictynna": Rifat is here playing on the fact that both Minos and Andreas are Cretan.

"The Gloss": the last line gestures toward the passage in *The Secret History* in which Procopius marvels at the empress Theodora's ability to "enjoy three men at once and satisfy them all," exploiting the orifices of the female body with élan. Theodora receives pride of place in two subsequent poems, "The Secret History" and "Temenos."

"The Black Book": Orhan Pamuk, Turkey's most celebrated contemporary novelist, published his *The Black Book* in 1990. Rifat is here playing with the name "Ruya," which means "dream" and is the name of the missing wife in the story.

"Blue Mountain.com": Blue Mountain is a worldwide e-commerce firm selling greeting cards over the Internet. It recently became the vehicle for an e-mail virus with particularly high Threat Metrics. The Kyrenia range in northern Cyprus is known locally as the Blue Mountains. Rifat informs me that she posted this poem to Karavis and he replied faulting her for mixing metaphors.

"A Question": the word "lickle" is a transliteration of a hapax legomenon that functions onomatopoeically in the original. The Turkish locative suffix for "in" in the last line is intentional and meant to contrast with the expected dative suffix for "to."

"Pantoum": Rifat and Karavis are both avid readers of Shakespeare. Allusions to as well as citations from the sonnets and the plays are scattered throughout *Pallikari*.

"Prime Minister of Cyprus:" Rifat is clearly referring to Rauf Denktash and to her previously expressed desire for a unified Cyprus. See "Untitled."

"The Apple": the Apple of Contention or Apple of Discord, inscribed *For the Fairest* and awarded by Paris to Aphrodite over her rival claimants Athena and Hera, was an indirect cause of the Trojan War.

ث

"Alcaics": the word "arsenic" derives from the Greek *arsenikos* (masculine, virile).

"The Way Ahead": Rifat moved to Cyprus in 1999 although her work as a translator from Greek and English documents for the Ministry of Foreign Affairs frequently takes her to Istanbul. She is still getting to know her new home, which accounts for the otherwise curious fact that the Lonely Planet travel guide (along with several other guidebooks) accompanies her on her occasional excursions around the island.

"Karaghiozis": Dionysis Savvopoulos, known as the Greek Bob Dylan, has attempted through his music to revive the Karaghiozis puppet theatre, a dying art form.

"From the 'Garland of Sulpicia'": This is a suite of five poems once thought to have been written by Tibullus and included as the fourth book of the *Corpus Tibullianum*. Its attribution to Sulpicia is now largely accepted by scholars of the period. The poem itself is a loose conflation and adaptation of the second and third elegies in the series.

"Wind": The reference here is undoubtedly to an early Karavis poem of the same title which begins, "Wind bangs like an angry landlord / hungry for rent" and includes the line "as if threatening to evict us." The Karavis poem deals with the relation between nature and culture whereas Rifat is clearly personalizing its theme. (The reader may be surprised to learn that it does indeed snow in the mountains of Cyprus.)

pallikari: brave man, hero, warrior; in Turkish, the word signifies "young man."

caique: boat, barque; pronounced with accent on the second syllable, "ka-í-ki."

rebetika: the music of the opium den, produced by the Greek refugees from Ionian Turkey after the war of 1922.

djoumboushi: Turkish for "feast," "banquet," naturalized in the Greek demotic. (The English word "banquet" is used in the original, requiring transposition.)

loukoumia: Turkish Delights.

Guzelyurt: the Turkish equivalent of the Greek *Morphou* (the beautiful place or country).

Mnasidika: the name of the young lesbian lover of Bilitis in Pierre Louÿs' 1894 collection of erotic poems, *The Songs of Bilitis*. The "blue-embroidered yellow robe" in "Sequel" is quoted from one of these, "Mnasidika's Silence."

temenos: temple, mosque.

Karaghiozis: the main character in the eponymous shadow/puppet theater which has become part of the cultural life of Greece. The word is a conflation of the Turkish roots for "dark" and "eye."

Anaphora Ston Andrea: a play on the title of Nikos Kazantzakis's memoir, *Anaphora Ston Greco* (*Report to Greco*); the terminal "s" is dropped in the dative.

David Solway is one of Canada's most highly respected poets and a famously iconoclastic social and cultural critic. A graduate of McGill and Concordia universities, he was a professor of English at John Abbott College, Montreal, a visiting faculty member at Brigham Young University, and writer-in-residence at Concordia University.

Solway is the author of numerous books, including *Modern Marriage*, which won the QSPELL Poetry Award; *Education Lost*, which won the QSPELL Non-Fiction Award; *Random Walks*, which was a finalist for Le Grand Prix du Livre de Montréal; and *Franklin's Passage*, which won the 2004 Grand Prix du Livre de Montréal. He publishes frequently in periodicals, including *The Atlantic Monthly, Books in Canada, The Fiddlehead, Canadian Literature, Descant, Journal of Modern Greek Studies, Parnassus, Partisan Review, Saturday Night, The Sewanee Review,* and *The Malahat Review*. He is a contributing editor at *Canadian Notes & Queries, and an associate editor for Books in Canada* and an occasional contributor to the book pages of *The National Post*. He lives in Hudson, Quebec, near Montreal.